AI & Blockchain for Climate Global Climate Solutions Insight on Sustainable Investments, Carbon Markets, and Green Bonds

Copyright

AI & Blockchain for Climate Finance: A Global Climate Solutions Insight on Sustainable Investments, Carbon Markets, and Green Bonds

ISBNs:

eBook: 978-1-991369-25-3

Paperback: 978-1-991369-26-0

Table of Contents

Executive Summary

The urgency of climate action requires innovative financial mechanisms to mobilize capital efficiently toward mitigation, adaptation, and sustainability projects. Traditional climate finance systems face challenges related to transparency, inefficiency, and accountability, limiting their impact. Emerging technologies, particularly Artificial Intelligence (AI) and Blockchain, are transforming how climate finance is managed, tracked, and allocated. AI enhances risk assessment, investment decision-making, and predictive analytics, while Blockchain ensures transparency, security, and efficiency in financial transactions, carbon markets, and sustainability-linked investments.

Key Themes and Their Relevance

AI and Blockchain are reshaping climate finance in three key ways:

1. **AI in Climate Finance**: AI enhances data-driven decision-making, investment optimization, and climate risk management. By analyzing large datasets, AI enables real-time financial insights, predictive modeling, and automated compliance tracking, ensuring capital flows are directed toward high-impact, sustainable projects.
2. **Blockchain for Transparency**: Blockchain improves the integrity of financial transactions by providing secure, immutable ledgers for carbon credit trading, green bond issuance, and decentralized climate finance platforms. By eliminating fraud and reducing inefficiencies, Blockchain enhances trust and verifiability in climate finance mechanisms.
3. **Integration of AI and Blockchain**: The synergy of AI and Blockchain strengthens financial accountability, investment security, and climate impact tracking. AI-driven automated compliance monitoring, smart contract execution, and AI-powered carbon credit verification enhance financial

efficiency, ensuring that climate finance is scalable, secure, and results-oriented.

By addressing existing gaps in financial oversight and climate investment flows, these technologies provide data-driven, transparent, and secure solutions to accelerate the transition to a low-carbon, resilient economy.

Summary of AI's Role in Climate Finance

AI optimizes risk assessment, improves climate-related investment strategies, and automates sustainability compliance tracking. It enhances carbon pricing, ESG investing, and emissions monitoring, ensuring data-driven financial decision-making. By leveraging machine learning and predictive analytics, AI enables climate finance stakeholders to identify high-impact opportunities and mitigate financial and environmental risks efficiently.

Summary of Blockchain's Role in Climate Finance

Blockchain enhances trust, transparency, and efficiency in climate finance by securing transactions, verifying carbon credits, and improving green bond accountability. Its decentralized structure eliminates fraud, double counting, and inefficiencies in climate finance reporting. Smart contracts further automate fund disbursement and compliance tracking, ensuring that climate investments deliver measurable environmental benefits.

Final Impact Statement on Policy and Technology

Maximizing AI and Blockchain's potential in climate finance requires clear governance frameworks, regulatory oversight, and cross-sector collaboration to ensure scalability, security, and long-term financial and environmental impact.

Introduction

The urgency of climate action has intensified the need for effective, transparent, and scalable financial mechanisms to support mitigation and adaptation efforts. Climate finance plays a critical role in funding renewable energy, carbon markets, and resilience projects, yet traditional financial systems face challenges such as inefficiencies, lack of transparency, and slow capital mobilization. Emerging technologies, particularly AI and Blockchain, are transforming climate finance by addressing these gaps and improving financial flows toward sustainable, high-impact projects.

AI enhances climate finance by enabling data-driven decision-making, risk assessment, and predictive analytics. Machine learning algorithms process vast amounts of climate and financial data, allowing investors, policymakers, and institutions to optimize resource allocation, forecast climate risks, and assess the financial viability of green investments. AI-driven insights enhance carbon pricing models, green bond markets, and sustainability-linked lending, making climate finance more efficient and targeted.

Blockchain improves accountability, security, and transparency in climate finance transactions. By leveraging decentralized ledgers and smart contracts, Blockchain ensures that carbon credits, green bonds, and climate funding flows are traceable, verifiable, and fraud-resistant. Tokenization further enables fractional investments in climate solutions, increasing accessibility and investor participation.

This Insight explores how AI and Blockchain are revolutionizing climate finance, highlighting key applications, policy considerations, and future directions for these transformative technologies.

Chapter 1: AI-Powered Decision-Making in Climate Finance

The growing complexity of climate finance requires advanced data-driven solutions to optimize investment decisions, assess financial risks, and enhance the efficiency of sustainable finance mechanisms. AI is transforming climate finance by enabling predictive modeling, risk assessment, and automated decision-making, ensuring that capital is directed toward high-impact, climate-resilient projects.

AI enhances risk analysis, carbon pricing, and ESG (Environmental, Social, and Governance) investing, allowing financial institutions, investors, and policymakers to evaluate climate-related financial risks, optimize carbon markets, and improve sustainable investment strategies. By leveraging machine learning, AI can process large volumes of financial, climate, and policy data, improving the accuracy and efficiency of credit scoring, green bond issuance, and emissions tracking.

This chapter explores how AI-driven analytics optimize financial flows, enhance decision-making in carbon markets, and improve sustainability-linked investment strategies. It also examines policy considerations, regulatory challenges, and ethical concerns in AI-driven climate finance, highlighting the role of AI in shaping a more efficient, transparent, and impactful financial ecosystem for climate action.

1.1 AI-Driven Risk Assessment in Climate Finance

Effective risk assessment is essential in climate finance, ensuring that investments are allocated to projects that offer both financial stability and positive environmental impact. Climate-related risks can be broadly categorized into physical risks and transition risks, both of which influence financial decision-making and the long-term viability of climate investments. AI-driven analytics play a crucial role in enhancing risk identification, predictive modeling, and financial assessment, improving the accuracy and efficiency of climate finance strategies.

1.1.1 Physical and Transition Risk Analysis

Physical risks in climate finance refer to the direct consequences of climate change, such as extreme weather events, rising sea levels, droughts, and heatwaves, which can disrupt economic activities and lead to financial losses. Traditional risk assessment methods often rely on historical data, which may not accurately capture the evolving nature of climate change. AI-powered models, leveraging satellite imagery, weather forecasts, and big data analytics, can predict climate-related disasters with greater precision. These models help financial institutions assess the potential impact of extreme events on infrastructure, supply chains, and asset values, allowing investors to price climate risks more effectively.

Transition risks, on the other hand, stem from the economic and regulatory shifts associated with the transition to a low-carbon economy. Changes in climate policies, carbon pricing mechanisms, and investor preferences can impact the profitability and viability of businesses, particularly in high-emission sectors. AI-driven analytics evaluate market trends, regulatory changes, and corporate climate disclosures, enabling investors to anticipate and mitigate financial risks linked to climate transition policies. By integrating real-time policy analysis and sustainability metrics, AI enhances financial decision-making and ensures that capital is directed toward climate-resilient investments.

1.1.2 AI-Driven Credit Scoring and Sustainable Investments

AI is revolutionizing credit scoring and investment assessment in climate finance by providing more comprehensive, real-time evaluations of financial and environmental risks. Traditional credit scoring models often focus on financial metrics alone, overlooking climate-related vulnerabilities that can affect an entity's long-term stability. AI-powered credit scoring incorporates non-traditional data sources, such as energy consumption patterns, climate risk exposure, and ESG performance, offering a more holistic evaluation of investment opportunities.

AI-driven credit models help financial institutions assess the creditworthiness of green projects and sustainability-linked loans, ensuring that funding is allocated to projects with strong environmental and financial performance. These models leverage machine learning algorithms to analyze vast datasets, improving risk predictions and reducing default probabilities.

In the green bond market, AI enhances the assessment of issuer credibility, project impact, and compliance with sustainability targets. By automating the evaluation process, AI enables faster and more reliable decision-making, ensuring that green finance instruments are transparent, accountable, and aligned with climate objectives.

Furthermore, AI facilitates sustainability-linked investing by identifying companies and projects that meet climate resilience criteria. By processing data from sustainability reports, climate disclosures, and financial statements, AI assists investors in allocating capital to initiatives that contribute to climate adaptation and mitigation goals.

As climate finance continues to evolve, AI-driven risk assessment tools will play an increasingly critical role in ensuring that investments are both financially sound and environmentally sustainable. However, the responsible deployment of AI requires strong regulatory frameworks and ethical considerations to minimize bias, ensure transparency, and maximize the effectiveness of AI-powered decision-making in climate finance.

1.2 AI in Carbon Markets and Emissions Trading

Carbon markets and emissions trading systems (ETS) are essential mechanisms for reducing greenhouse gas (GHG) emissions by placing a financial cost on carbon pollution. These systems rely on accurate pricing, efficient trading, and transparent monitoring of emissions reductions. However, traditional carbon markets face challenges such as price volatility, regulatory complexity, and data discrepancies. AI is playing a transformative role in optimizing carbon pricing, improving market efficiency, and enhancing emissions monitoring, making carbon trading more effective and credible.

1.2.1 Optimizing Carbon Pricing and Market Dynamics

Effective carbon pricing is critical for incentivizing businesses to reduce emissions and invest in low-carbon technologies. However, setting accurate carbon prices is complex, as it requires considering market supply and demand, regulatory policies, and economic conditions. AI-driven models address these challenges by analyzing historical carbon price trends, emissions data, and macroeconomic indicators to predict carbon price fluctuations more accurately.

Machine learning algorithms process vast datasets in real time, allowing policymakers and market participants to anticipate price shifts and adjust trading strategies accordingly. This helps reduce market volatility and improves the predictability of carbon pricing mechanisms, ensuring that carbon credits reflect true environmental costs. AI-powered risk assessment models also assist companies in developing carbon risk management strategies, enabling them to adjust investment decisions based on projected carbon price trends.

Additionally, AI enhances automated carbon trading platforms, improving the efficiency of emissions trading markets. These platforms use AI-driven algorithms to match buyers and sellers, optimize transaction timing, and detect fraudulent activities in carbon credit trading. By increasing market liquidity and reducing inefficiencies, AI contributes to a more stable, transparent, and cost-effective carbon trading ecosystem.

1.2.2 AI for Real-Time Emissions Monitoring

Accurate and reliable emissions monitoring is fundamental to the integrity of carbon markets. Traditional emissions reporting often relies on self-reported data, which can be subject to inaccuracies or misrepresentation. AI is addressing these challenges by enabling real-time emissions tracking through advanced monitoring systems, ensuring that emissions reductions are verifiable and traceable.

AI-powered satellite imaging and remote sensing technologies enhance emissions monitoring by analyzing atmospheric data and detecting pollution patterns from industrial sites, transportation networks, and deforestation activities. These technologies provide real-time, high-resolution emissions data, allowing regulators to verify that carbon credits are backed by genuine emissions reductions.

Furthermore, AI-driven Internet of Things (IoT) sensors installed at industrial facilities track emissions output in real time, automatically flagging deviations from regulatory limits. By integrating machine learning algorithms, these systems can predict emissions trends and suggest mitigation measures, improving compliance with carbon reduction commitments.

AI also strengthens carbon offset validation by assessing reforestation, afforestation, and soil carbon sequestration projects. By analyzing climate data, land use changes, and carbon absorption rates, AI helps determine the actual carbon sequestration potential of nature-based solutions. This ensures that carbon offsets are credible and aligned with global emissions reduction goals.

By improving emissions monitoring, AI enhances the integrity of carbon markets, reducing the risk of double counting, fraud, and misreporting. As carbon markets continue to expand, AI-driven solutions will be critical in ensuring accuracy, accountability, and efficiency, ultimately strengthening the role of emissions trading in global climate action.

1.3 AI-Enhanced ESG Investing and Sustainable Finance

Environmental, Social, and Governance (ESG) investing has become a cornerstone of sustainable finance, guiding capital toward projects and companies that demonstrate strong sustainability commitments. However, traditional ESG assessments often face challenges related to data inconsistency, subjectivity, and greenwashing risks. AI is playing a pivotal role in enhancing ESG investment strategies by providing data-driven insights, real-time monitoring, and predictive analytics, ensuring that investments align with environmental and financial sustainability goals.

1.3.1 AI-Driven ESG Analytics

AI is revolutionizing ESG analytics by processing vast amounts of structured and unstructured data, improving the accuracy and reliability of sustainability assessments. Traditional ESG evaluations rely on company-reported data, which can be inconsistent or influenced by subjective ratings. AI enhances this process by:

• Analyzing real-time data from sustainability reports, climate disclosures, news articles, and social media to assess corporate ESG performance.

• Detecting greenwashing risks through natural language processing (NLP), identifying inconsistencies between corporate statements and actual sustainability practices.

• Generating predictive ESG scores based on historical data, regulatory trends, and industry benchmarks, allowing investors to assess long-term sustainability risks.

By automating ESG analysis, AI enables investors to identify high-performing sustainable assets, optimize investment portfolios, and ensure regulatory compliance. This strengthens ESG integration into mainstream finance, ensuring transparency, accountability, and measurable environmental impact.

1.3.2 AI for Green Bond Market Development

Green bonds have emerged as a key financial instrument for funding climate-related projects, yet challenges such as impact verification, risk assessment, and inconsistent reporting standards remain. AI is addressing these challenges by improving green bond issuance, impact assessment, and market predictions.

• **Automated impact tracking**: AI processes real-time environmental data to verify whether projects funded by green bonds meet their sustainability commitments.

• **Enhanced risk assessment**: AI-powered models evaluate the financial and environmental risks associated with green bonds, helping investors make informed decisions.

• **Market forecasting**: Machine learning algorithms analyze macroeconomic trends and investor sentiment to predict demand for green bonds, improving market stability.

By leveraging AI, the green bond market can scale more effectively, ensuring that climate finance flows toward verified, high-impact projects, reducing risks and increasing investor confidence.

1.4 Challenges and Policy Considerations for AI in Climate Finance

While AI offers transformative benefits for climate finance, its widespread adoption raises ethical, governance, and regulatory challenges that must be addressed to ensure transparency, fairness, and accountability. Effective policies and collaboration between governments, financial institutions, and technology providers are essential to maximize AI's potential while mitigating risks.

1.4.1 Ethical and Governance Concerns

AI-driven climate finance models rely on vast datasets and machine learning algorithms, which, if not properly regulated, may introduce bias, privacy risks, and accountability issues. Key concerns include:

• **Algorithmic bias**: AI models trained on incomplete or biased datasets may result in discriminatory investment decisions, excluding vulnerable communities from access to climate finance.

• **Lack of transparency**: AI decision-making processes are often complex and opaque, making it difficult for investors and regulators to validate financial predictions and risk assessments.

• **Data privacy risks**: The collection and processing of financial and climate data must comply with global data protection laws to prevent misuse or unauthorized access.

Addressing these concerns requires clear regulatory frameworks, ethical AI guidelines, and continuous oversight to ensure that AI in climate finance remains inclusive, fair, and secure.

1.4.2 Public-Private Partnerships for AI Adoption

Scaling AI-driven climate finance solutions requires strong collaboration between governments, financial institutions, and technology providers. Public-private partnerships (PPPs) can:

• **Facilitate regulatory alignment**: Governments can establish AI governance frameworks to ensure that AI applications in climate finance comply with global sustainability standards.

• **Support AI innovation**: Investments in research and development (R&D) can drive the creation of AI-powered tools that improve risk assessment, investment decisions, and emissions monitoring.

• **Enhance capacity-building**: Financial professionals must be trained in AI-driven climate finance analytics to maximize the effectiveness of these technologies.

By fostering cross-sector collaboration, AI can be deployed responsibly, improving climate finance efficiency while maintaining financial integrity and environmental accountability.

Chapter 2: Blockchain for Transparency and Efficiency in Climate Finance

Ensuring transparency, efficiency, and accountability in climate finance is essential for mobilizing capital toward sustainable projects. Traditional financial mechanisms often face challenges such as fraud, double counting of carbon credits, and inefficiencies in fund distribution. Blockchain technology is emerging as a powerful tool to enhance trust, streamline transactions, and provide verifiable records of climate finance flows.

By leveraging decentralized ledgers, smart contracts, and tokenization, Blockchain enables secure, tamper-proof tracking of carbon credits, green bonds, and sustainability-linked investments. This technology improves the integrity of carbon markets, climate adaptation funds, and international finance mechanisms, ensuring that investments deliver measurable environmental benefits.

This chapter explores how Blockchain is transforming climate finance by reducing fraud, increasing transparency, and improving financial accountability. It examines its applications in carbon credit trading, green bond tracking, and decentralized finance (DeFi) for climate investments while addressing the regulatory challenges and policy considerations necessary for its widespread adoption.

2.1 Blockchain as a Trust Mechanism in Climate Finance

Trust and transparency are fundamental to the effective deployment of climate finance. However, traditional financial mechanisms often suffer from inefficiencies, lack of accountability, and risks of misallocation of funds. Blockchain technology offers a decentralized and tamper-proof system that enhances transparency, automates transactions, and ensures that funds are allocated efficiently and used as intended. By leveraging decentralized ledgers, smart contracts, and tokenization, Blockchain provides a robust framework for tracking climate finance transactions, reducing fraud, and increasing investor confidence.

2.1.1 Decentralized Ledgers for Climate Finance Transactions

A major challenge in climate finance is the lack of transparency in fund distribution. Many climate finance mechanisms involve multiple stakeholders, including governments, private investors, multilateral institutions, and project developers. This complexity often leads to misreporting, inefficiencies, and limited accountability.

Blockchain technology addresses this challenge through decentralized ledgers, which provide an immutable and transparent record of all financial transactions. These ledgers ensure that every transaction, whether related to carbon credit trading, green bond issuance, or sustainability-linked investments, is verifiable, tamper-proof, and traceable.

• **Enhanced transparency**: Blockchain records financial transactions on a distributed ledger, making data available to all relevant stakeholders in real time. This minimizes the risk of fraud, double counting, and misallocation of funds.

• **Efficiency in fund transfers**: Traditional climate finance transactions often involve intermediaries, leading to delays, additional costs, and inefficiencies. Blockchain streamlines these transactions by enabling direct peer-to-peer fund transfers, reducing administrative overhead.

• **Trust and accountability**: Since Blockchain records cannot be altered, all financial flows remain auditable and traceable, ensuring that climate funds are used effectively. This enhances investor confidence and encourages more private capital to be directed toward climate action.

Decentralized ledgers eliminate the reliance on centralized institutions, making climate finance more efficient, secure, and trustworthy.

2.1.2 Smart Contracts for Automated Climate Finance Disbursement

Smart contracts are self-executing digital contracts that automate financial transactions based on predefined conditions. In climate finance, they reduce administrative burdens, eliminate manual errors, and enhance efficiency in fund disbursement.

• **Automatic fund release**: Smart contracts ensure that funds are only disbursed when specific sustainability criteria are met. For example, a green bond investment for a renewable energy project may be automatically released upon verification that the project has achieved its targeted emissions reduction.

• **Eliminating intermediaries**: By automating transactions, smart contracts remove the need for third-party validation, reducing costs and enhancing efficiency.

• **Enforcing compliance**: Smart contracts can be programmed to ensure that climate finance projects adhere to sustainability reporting standards. If a project fails to meet its environmental commitments, payments can be withheld or redirected.

By enabling automated, transparent, and efficient fund distribution, smart contracts help ensure that climate finance reaches its intended purpose without delays or financial mismanagement.

2.1.3 Tokenization of Carbon Credits and Climate Bonds

Tokenization refers to the process of converting real-world assets into digital tokens on a Blockchain, making them more accessible, tradable, and secure.

• **Carbon credits**: Blockchain enables the creation of digital carbon credits, which can be securely tracked and traded on decentralized marketplaces, reducing the risk of double counting and fraud.

• **Green bonds**: Tokenization allows fractional ownership of green bonds, making them accessible to a broader range of investors, improving liquidity in sustainable finance markets.

By digitizing climate finance assets, Blockchain enhances transparency, enables real-time tracking of financial flows, and facilitates broader participation in climate investments.

2.2 Blockchain in Carbon Credit Markets & Climate Bonds

Carbon credit markets and green bonds play a crucial role in financing climate action. However, these financial mechanisms often face challenges related to transparency, verification, and accountability. Issues such as double counting of carbon credits, unclear tracking of green bond proceeds, and limited access to climate investment opportunities can undermine their effectiveness. Blockchain technology offers secure, immutable, and decentralized solutions to address these concerns, ensuring that climate finance flows efficiently and is used for its intended purpose.

2.2.1 Addressing Double Counting and Ensuring Credit Integrity

Carbon credit markets are designed to provide financial incentives for organizations to reduce their greenhouse gas (GHG) emissions. However, traditional carbon trading systems lack transparency and reliability, leading to risks such as double counting, where the same emissions reduction is claimed multiple times by different entities. This undermines the credibility of carbon offset markets and reduces investor confidence.

Blockchain technology addresses this issue by creating a decentralized and immutable record of carbon credit transactions, ensuring that each credit is uniquely identified and verifiable. Key benefits include:

• **Transparent tracking**: Blockchain registers each carbon credit with a unique digital identifier, preventing duplication and ensuring accurate tracking of emissions reductions.

• **Automated verification**: Smart contracts enable automated validation of carbon credits, ensuring that they meet verified sustainability standards before being traded.

• **Real-time auditing**: Stakeholders, including regulators and investors, can access Blockchain-based real-time data on carbon credit issuance, transfers, and retirements, ensuring full accountability.

• **Eliminating fraud**: By removing the reliance on centralized intermediaries, Blockchain ensures that carbon credits are issued, traded, and retired with complete transparency.

By integrating Blockchain into carbon credit markets, emissions trading becomes more credible, traceable, and resistant to manipulation, ultimately driving greater participation and investment in emissions reduction efforts.

2.2.2 Blockchain's Role in Tracking Green Bond Proceeds

Green bonds are financial instruments specifically designed to fund projects with environmental benefits, such as renewable energy, sustainable agriculture, and water conservation. However, one of the major challenges in green bond markets is ensuring that funds are used as intended and that investors can track the environmental impact of their investments.

Blockchain enhances green bond transparency by:

• **Providing immutable transaction records**: Every financial transaction related to a green bond issuance is recorded on Blockchain, ensuring that the flow of funds is traceable and tamper-proof.

• **Automating compliance**: Smart contracts enforce green bond commitments, automatically triggering disbursements only when sustainability milestones are met.

• **Real-time impact tracking**: Blockchain enables real-time monitoring of green bond-funded projects, providing investors with accurate, verifiable data on environmental performance.

By improving accountability and reducing risks of misallocation, Blockchain strengthens investor confidence in green bonds as a reliable climate finance tool.

2.2.3 DeFi Applications in Climate Investment

DeFi is emerging as a game-changer in climate investment, providing peer-to-peer lending, automated investment strategies, and global accessibility to climate finance.

• **Tokenized green assets**: DeFi platforms enable the fractional ownership of climate-focused financial instruments, such as renewable energy investments and carbon offset projects.

• **Automated lending and borrowing**: Smart contracts facilitate transparent, automated lending for climate projects, reducing reliance on traditional financial institutions.

• **Global accessibility**: DeFi platforms democratize climate finance, allowing individuals and institutions worldwide to invest in sustainable projects without intermediaries.

By integrating DeFi into climate finance, Blockchain helps scale sustainable investments, ensuring that capital reaches high-impact climate solutions efficiently and transparently.

2.3 Regulatory & Implementation Challenges

While Blockchain offers enhanced transparency, security, and efficiency in climate finance, its widespread adoption faces regulatory and implementation challenges. Ensuring compliance with financial regulations, integrating Blockchain with traditional banking systems, and securing government and multilateral support are critical for the successful deployment of this technology in climate finance. Addressing these challenges will be essential to maximize Blockchain's potential while maintaining financial stability, investor confidence, and legal compliance.

2.3.1 Compliance with Financial Regulations

Blockchain-based climate finance solutions must adhere to existing financial regulations, anti-money laundering (AML) laws, and Know Your Customer (KYC) requirements. Traditional finance is governed by strict regulatory frameworks designed to prevent fraud, protect investors, and ensure market stability. However, the decentralized nature of Blockchain presents unique challenges:

• **Regulatory uncertainty**: Many jurisdictions lack clear guidelines on the legal status of Blockchain-based financial transactions, particularly in carbon trading and green bonds. Uncertainty around regulatory compliance can hinder adoption.

• **AML and KYC requirements**: DeFi and Blockchain-based transactions often provide pseudonymity, which conflicts with AML and KYC regulations. Ensuring compliance while maintaining Blockchain's decentralized structure remains a key challenge.

• **Cross-border complexities**: Climate finance is often international, requiring alignment between different countries' regulatory frameworks. The lack of standardized Blockchain regulations complicates cross-border transactions, making it difficult for global carbon markets and green bonds to function efficiently.

To overcome these challenges, regulators must develop clear guidelines on Blockchain's role in financial transactions, ensuring that its application in climate finance aligns with global financial standards while maintaining the transparency and efficiency that Blockchain provides.

2.3.2 Integration Barriers with Traditional Banking

Despite its benefits, Blockchain technology faces significant integration challenges with the traditional banking and financial system. Many financial institutions are hesitant to adopt Blockchain due to concerns over technological compatibility, regulatory compliance, and operational disruption. Key barriers include:

• **Legacy banking infrastructure**: Traditional financial institutions operate on centralized, regulated frameworks, which contrast with Blockchain's decentralized, permissionless nature. Aligning these systems requires substantial investment in technological upgrades and regulatory adaptation.

• **Institutional reluctance**: Banks and financial institutions often resist Blockchain adoption due to concerns over disintermediation, where Blockchain-based finance reduces their role in fund transfers, lending, and investment tracking.

• **Scalability concerns**: Many Blockchain networks face transaction speed and scalability limitations, which can be a challenge for processing large-scale financial transactions efficiently.

For successful integration, hybrid financial models combining Blockchain's transparency with traditional banking regulations need to be developed. Collaboration between banks, financial regulators, and Blockchain developers can facilitate the adoption of Blockchain-based climate finance solutions without disrupting existing financial stability.

2.3.3 Government and Multilateral Support for Blockchain-Based Finance

The role of governments and multilateral organizations is critical in scaling Blockchain applications in climate finance. Public sector involvement can help standardize regulations, provide investment incentives, and foster international cooperation. Key areas of support include:

• **Regulatory harmonization**: Governments and international organizations must develop consistent global standards for Blockchain applications in climate finance, ensuring cross-border interoperability and legal clarity.

• **Public funding and incentives**: Government grants and financial incentives can accelerate the adoption of Blockchain for carbon credit markets, green bonds, and emissions tracking, reducing barriers for private sector investment.

• **Capacity building**: Multilateral organizations such as the United Nations (UN), the World Bank, and the International Monetary Fund (IMF) can support Blockchain adoption by providing technical guidance, conducting pilot projects, and fostering collaboration between public and private sectors.

By securing strong government backing and international regulatory alignment, Blockchain can be integrated into climate finance at scale, ensuring long-term financial stability, transparency, and efficiency in funding climate action.

Chapter 3: The Future of AI and Blockchain Integration in Climate Finance

As the demand for scalable, transparent, and efficient climate finance solutions grows, the integration of AI and Blockchain is poised to transform the way capital is mobilized for climate action. While both technologies offer significant individual benefits—AI enhances predictive analytics and investment decision-making, while Blockchain ensures transparency and trust—their combined application presents new opportunities to optimize financial mechanisms for sustainability.

The convergence of AI and Blockchain can enhance the security, automation, and efficiency of climate finance by enabling real-time risk assessment, automated carbon credit verification, and streamlined green bond issuance. These synergies will help overcome existing gaps in financial accountability, impact measurement, and fund distribution, ensuring that capital flows are directed toward high-impact, verifiable climate projects.

This chapter explores the emerging opportunities and challenges of integrating AI and Blockchain in climate finance. It examines their potential to scale investment in climate solutions, strengthen compliance mechanisms, and drive innovation in green finance. Additionally, it highlights the policy considerations, regulatory frameworks, and long-term implications of these technologies in shaping the future of climate finance.

3.1 AI & Blockchain Synergies for Smarter Climate Investments

The integration of AI and Blockchain is transforming climate finance by improving risk assessment, transparency, and efficiency. While AI provides advanced analytics, predictive modeling, and automation, Blockchain ensures secure, tamper-proof transactions and accountability. Together, these technologies are enhancing financial decision-making, optimizing carbon markets, and strengthening investment security.

By combining AI's ability to process large datasets with Blockchain's decentralized ledger system, climate finance can become more efficient, verifiable, and scalable. Key applications include AI-driven climate risk modeling, automated carbon credit issuance, and smart contracts for climate fund allocation.

3.1.1 AI-Driven Climate Risk Models with Blockchain

Accurately assessing climate-related financial risks is essential for directing investments toward resilient, sustainable projects. AI-driven climate risk models use machine learning and big data analytics to analyze patterns in weather trends, emissions data, and financial market fluctuations. These models help investors and policymakers:

• **Predict climate risks**: AI can assess the likelihood of extreme weather events, resource shortages, and regulatory changes affecting financial assets.

• **Optimize investment strategies**: Machine learning algorithms evaluate historical financial performance, ESG data, and sustainability metrics to guide low-carbon investment decisions.

• **Enhance risk mitigation**: AI models identify early warning signs of environmental risks, enabling financial institutions to adjust portfolios and mitigate losses.

By integrating AI-driven climate risk assessments with Blockchain, data security and traceability are improved. Risk models and financial transactions can be recorded on a decentralized ledger, ensuring tamper-proof, verifiable risk analyses that enhance investor confidence.

3.1.2 Automated Carbon Credit Issuance and Verification

The carbon credit market plays a vital role in incentivizing emissions reductions, but challenges such as double counting, fraud, and lack of verification undermine its effectiveness. AI and Blockchain together automate carbon credit issuance and ensure integrity by:

• **AI-driven emissions tracking**: Machine learning algorithms analyze satellite imagery, IoT sensor data, and industrial emissions reports to verify actual reductions in carbon output.

• **Blockchain-based carbon credit registry**: Each verified carbon credit is digitally tokenized on a Blockchain, ensuring that credits are unique, traceable, and immutable.

• **Fraud prevention and accountability**: AI detects inconsistencies in emissions data, while Blockchain ensures that credits cannot be duplicated or manipulated.

This integration streamlines carbon trading markets, making them more transparent and efficient while reducing administrative costs and enhancing regulatory compliance.

3.1.3 AI-Enhanced Smart Contracts for Funding Allocation

AI-powered smart contracts are revolutionizing climate finance disbursement by automating investment agreements, tracking sustainability milestones, and ensuring compliance with environmental commitments.

• **Automated fund disbursement**: AI-driven smart contracts execute payments only when predefined sustainability targets are met, reducing financial mismanagement.

• **Data-driven compliance tracking**: AI continuously monitors green project performance using real-time sustainability data, ensuring that climate finance is used as intended.

• **Enhanced financial accountability**: Blockchain records all smart contract transactions, providing an audit trail for investors and regulators.

By integrating AI and Blockchain in climate finance, smart contracts enable secure, transparent, and automated fund allocation, ensuring that climate investments achieve measurable environmental impact.

3.2 Scaling AI & Blockchain for Global Climate Finance

The integration of AI and Blockchain is revolutionizing global climate finance by enhancing efficiency, transparency, and accountability. As governments, financial institutions, and investors seek to scale sustainable finance, AI and Blockchain offer solutions that enable real-time compliance tracking, accurate climate impact assessments, and seamless data-sharing across stakeholders. These technologies help reduce fraud, improve risk assessment, and accelerate capital flows into climate adaptation and mitigation projects.

By leveraging automated compliance mechanisms, verifiable impact tracking, and decentralized data-sharing, AI and Blockchain are making climate finance more scalable, accessible, and outcome-driven.

3.2.1 Automated Sustainability Compliance Tracking

One of the major challenges in global climate finance is ensuring that funds are allocated to projects that genuinely contribute to emissions reduction and environmental sustainability. Many climate finance mechanisms, including green bonds, carbon credits, and sustainability-linked loans, require ongoing monitoring to ensure compliance with sustainability commitments. However, traditional compliance tracking methods rely on manual reporting and third-party audits, which can be time-consuming, costly, and prone to inaccuracies.

AI and Blockchain address these challenges by automating sustainability compliance tracking through:

• **AI-powered monitoring systems**: Machine learning algorithms analyze satellite imagery, industrial emissions data, and corporate sustainability reports to verify compliance with green finance commitments.

• **Blockchain-based compliance records**: Once compliance data is verified by AI, it is recorded on a Blockchain ledger, ensuring immutability, transparency, and auditability.

• **Smart contract enforcement**: AI-driven smart contracts trigger automatic fund disbursement or penalties based on compliance outcomes, reducing the risk of financial mismanagement.

By automating sustainability compliance tracking, AI and Blockchain increase regulatory oversight, improve investor confidence, and ensure that climate finance achieves its intended environmental benefits.

3.2.2 AI-Based Climate Impact Assessments with Blockchain Verification

Assessing the long-term impact of climate finance projects is critical for ensuring accountability and effectiveness. Traditional impact assessment models struggle with inconsistent data sources, delayed reporting, and a lack of standardized metrics. AI and Blockchain solve these challenges by providing accurate, real-time impact tracking with verifiable records.

• **AI-driven impact assessment models**: Machine learning algorithms analyze historical climate data, financial transactions, and real-world environmental indicators to predict the long-term effectiveness of funded projects.

• **Blockchain for verification**: AI-generated impact assessments are securely recorded on Blockchain, preventing data manipulation and enabling transparent, tamper-proof reporting.

• **Automated climate performance scoring**: AI assigns sustainability scores to funded projects based on energy efficiency, emissions reduction, and biodiversity impact, allowing investors and regulators to make data-driven decisions.

By integrating AI-driven impact assessments with Blockchain verification, global climate finance can be more transparent, standardized, and results-oriented, ensuring that investments contribute meaningfully to climate resilience and sustainability goals.

3.2.3 Real-Time Data-Sharing Across Stakeholders

Effective climate finance requires seamless coordination between governments, financial institutions, investors, and environmental organizations. However, traditional data-sharing models are often fragmented, siloed, and inefficient. AI and Blockchain facilitate real-time, decentralized data-sharing, ensuring that all stakeholders have access to accurate, up-to-date climate finance information.

• AI automates data aggregation, collecting and processing climate finance metrics from multiple sources.

• Blockchain ensures secure, tamper-proof records, allowing regulators and investors to verify data integrity.

• Decentralized access enhances transparency, enabling stakeholders to make informed decisions without relying on centralized intermediaries.

By enhancing real-time data-sharing, AI and Blockchain improve collaboration, trust, and efficiency in global climate finance, helping to accelerate sustainable investments worldwide.

3.3 Policy & Future Considerations

The integration of AI and Blockchain into climate finance presents significant opportunities to enhance transparency, efficiency, and scalability. However, realizing the full potential of these technologies requires the development of robust governance frameworks, solutions to financial and technological barriers, and long-term strategies for sustainable adoption. Establishing clear policies and regulatory guidelines will be essential to ensuring that AI and Blockchain are deployed ethically, securely, and in alignment with global climate finance goals.

3.3.1 Governance Frameworks for AI-Blockchain Adoption

Governments and regulatory bodies play a critical role in shaping the governance frameworks needed for AI and Blockchain in climate finance. These frameworks must balance innovation with risk management, ensuring that technological advancements contribute positively to climate finance objectives without introducing systemic risks.

Key governance considerations include:

• **Regulatory clarity**: Many jurisdictions lack clear legal definitions and standards for Blockchain-based climate finance mechanisms. Policymakers must establish guidelines on digital asset classification, smart contract enforceability, and AI-driven financial decision-making.

• **Ethical AI implementation**: AI algorithms must be transparent, unbiased, and explainable, particularly in financial risk assessments and sustainability compliance tracking. Governance frameworks should include AI auditing mechanisms to prevent discriminatory or misleading outcomes.

• **Data security and privacy**: AI and Blockchain systems process vast amounts of climate finance data. Governments must enforce data protection laws to ensure secure storage, ethical data usage, and compliance with global privacy regulations.

• **Cross-border cooperation**: Climate finance operates on an international scale, requiring harmonized regulations that enable seamless AI-Blockchain adoption across different financial jurisdictions. Multilateral organizations such as the United Nations, World Bank, and IMF can facilitate standardized policies for global climate finance transparency.

By establishing structured governance frameworks, regulators can maximize the benefits of AI and Blockchain while minimizing risks related to fraud, regulatory uncertainty, and ethical concerns.

3.3.2 Overcoming Financial and Technological Barriers

Despite their potential, AI and Blockchain technologies face financial and technological barriers that limit their widespread adoption in climate finance. Addressing these challenges will be essential for scaling climate-focused financial solutions.

Key barriers and solutions include:

• **High implementation costs**: Deploying AI and Blockchain requires substantial investment in infrastructure, data management, and technical expertise. Public-private partnerships (PPPs) and government funding incentives can help reduce upfront costs for climate finance stakeholders.

• **Scalability issues**: Many Blockchain networks face transaction speed limitations, making them inefficient for high-volume financial transactions. Advances in Layer 2 scaling solutions, such as sidechains and off-chain processing, can improve Blockchain efficiency.

• **Integration with legacy systems**: Traditional financial institutions operate on centralized systems that may not be easily compatible with decentralized Blockchain frameworks. Hybrid models that combine traditional banking infrastructure with AI-Blockchain enhancements can facilitate gradual adoption.

• Digital divide and accessibility: Some regions, particularly in developing economies, may lack the technological infrastructure to support AI and Blockchain deployment. Expanding access to digital tools and financial literacy programs will be essential for ensuring equitable participation in climate finance.

By addressing these financial and technological barriers, AI and Blockchain can become widely accessible, cost-effective, and seamlessly integrated into climate finance ecosystems.

3.3.3 Long-Term Impact on Climate Finance

The long-term integration of AI and Blockchain in climate finance will reshape how capital is mobilized, managed, and monitored for sustainability. These technologies will drive:

• **Greater investment transparency**: Blockchain will ensure that climate finance transactions remain verifiable and fraud-resistant, increasing investor confidence.

• **Improved climate risk management**: AI-driven analytics will provide real-time insights into environmental risks, helping financial institutions make smarter, more resilient investment decisions.

• **Scalable global solutions**: AI and Blockchain will enable cross-border collaboration, harmonized carbon markets, and streamlined sustainability reporting, strengthening the effectiveness of international climate finance efforts.

As these technologies evolve, ongoing regulatory advancements, investment in digital infrastructure, and cross-sector collaboration will determine their success in transforming climate finance into a more transparent, accountable, and impactful system.

Conclusion

The integration of AI in climate finance is revolutionizing how financial risks are assessed, investments are allocated, and sustainability compliance is monitored. AI-driven predictive analytics, automated risk modeling, and real-time impact assessments are enhancing investment decision-making, improving carbon pricing mechanisms, and strengthening ESG investing. By processing large datasets efficiently, AI ensures that capital flows are directed toward high-impact climate projects, optimizing financial outcomes while supporting global climate goals.

Blockchain technology plays a crucial role in enhancing trust, transparency, and efficiency in climate finance. Through decentralized ledgers, smart contracts, and tokenization, Blockchain eliminates fraud, double counting, and inefficiencies in carbon markets and green bonds. By ensuring secure, verifiable financial transactions, Blockchain strengthens accountability and fosters greater investor confidence in sustainable finance mechanisms.

To maximize the benefits of AI and Blockchain in climate finance, clear policy frameworks and regulatory oversight are essential. Establishing global governance standards, ethical AI guidelines, and cross-border Blockchain regulations will ensure that these technologies operate securely, equitably, and in alignment with climate objectives while minimizing risks related to data privacy and financial stability.

As AI and Blockchain continue to evolve, their successful integration into climate finance will drive innovation, improve financial efficiency, and accelerate capital flows toward sustainable development, creating a more resilient, transparent, and scalable global climate finance ecosystem.

www.ingramcontent.com/pod-product-compliance
Lightning Source LLC
Chambersburg PA
CBHW070948210326
41520CB00021B/7114

9 781991 369260